A HORSE IS NOT A BICYCLE

Elizabeth Wiley

Order this book online at www.trafford.com
or email orders@trafford.com

Most Trafford titles are also available at major online book retailers.

Trafford
PUBLISHING® www.trafford.com
North America & international
toll-free: 844 688 6899 (USA & Canada)
fax: 812 355 4082

Our mission is to efficiently provide the world's finest, most comprehensive book publishing
service, enabling every author to experience success. To find out how to publish your book,
your way, and have it available worldwide, visit us online at www.trafford.com

Because of the dynamic nature of the Internet, any web addresses or links contained in
this book may have changed since publication and may no longer be valid. The views
expressed in this work are solely those of the author and do not necessarily reflect the views
of the publisher, and the publisher hereby disclaims any responsibility for them.

ISBN: 978-1-6987-0977-2 (sc)
978-1-6987-0978-9 (e)

Print information available on the last page.

Trafford rev. 10/28/2021

A Horse is NOT a Bicycle

Teaching your Child how to partner with animals-and be responsible for them BEFORE letting them have one. FOREVER HOMES

INTRODUCTION

Our books are written as on ongoing series for high risk youth, veterans, and first responders as well as their parents and those who are raising them.

One of the reasons for starting this series was we, as special needs teachers, as therapists, as Directors of programs and private schools for high risk youth began to recognize how many of the children and youth were children of veterans, grandchildren of veterans, and also first responders.

We then noticed the numbers of minority children and poverty level financial back grounds were the reality for high risk children and youth. We saw children of Mothers who had been as young as NINE at the birth of their child among the high risk students. Whether rich, or poverty level, we saw children of alcohol, sexual, and drug addictions.

We saw children as young as 18 months labeled with an alphabet of mental health disorders, medicated and put into "special schools" where in fact media found they were often warehoused, abused, and not taught at all. Upon seeing a news story about the schools discovered at some of the licensed sites, in which children and teens often did not have desks, or chairs to sit on, let alone proper educational supplies and equipment for special learning program, we joined with others, and designed programs.

We were naive enough to think our work, offered FREE in most cases, would be welcomed especially as we offer it free and often through research projects, but, it was NOT valued or wanted.

What? we asked?

We went back to college and while earning degrees we had apparently NOT needed while working with children of the very rich in expensive private schools, we did research projects to document our findings. To find ways to overcome the problems. Again, our work was NOT valued or wanted.

One of our associates, who had asked many of us to volunteer in a once a month FREE reading program in the local public schools, was held back for almost two years doing paperwork and proving her volunteers, most of them parents of successful children, teens and adults, could read a first five years book and teach parents how to read those books to their own children. She was a Deputy United States Prosecutor, and had recruited friends from all levels of law enforcement, child and family services, education and volunteer groups that served children and families.

None the less, we continued our work, met a fabulous and expensive Psychiatrist who was building his own server system and the first online education project after creating a massive and encompassing medical examination study guide for graduate medical students to assist them in passing global and national medical examinations for licensing.

We worked with a team of citizens and specialists in education who had created a 39 manual project for students, parents and teachers to be able to learn on their own.

This series of books includes ideas, history and thoughts from the students, the parents, and professionals who work with these situations.

Jesus was told, don't have children wasting your time, and he responded, let the children come.

Our work is to bring children to us, and to those who have the heart and love to develop the uniqueness and individuality of each of God's creations. Many of them are of different religions, and beliefs, and many are atheists but believe fully in the wonder and uniqueness of every human.

To all who have helped and continue to help children and anyone wanting to learn, we thank God and we thank you.

Chapter One

Introduction

This book if for those who want an animal, or who have a child who wants an animal. Legally a child is 18 or under. Legally, if you give your child an animal and it is abused, abandoned, or mistreated, YOU are the one the animal police will come after and fine, or jail.

One day, in my forties, I went to visit my Dad. I had left training and was now running an equine therapy program for high risk youth, veterans, first responders and their families. My Dad said to me how proud he was of my having made my dreams and goals with horses come true. He then said that he loved horses, always wanted to ride, but was just a bit too self preserving to get in the saddle.

WHAT! I told him I had always thought it was my Dad who gave me my start and love of horses.

He said he had taken me to the pony rides at Griffith Park in Los Angeles before I was six months old, while visiting my Grandparents in nearby Pasadena. I could easily see how my Dad holding me on the saddle of that tiny pony might have given me the peace, joy and confidence of all my riding years.

My Dad also told me of a time when my Mom was visiting a relatives ranch, and did not notice I had wandered off, possibly age four, into the corn fields. This particular ranch was hundreds of acres wide. Soon the neighbors, and anyone with a horse was out looking for me. It took all night.

My memory of this was the corn, darkness, and waking up to looking up horse legs into a horse face and someone shouting. My Dad rushing to claim me. Horses of course again were a huge part of my Dad, and peace and care in my life.

When my sixteen year old son was diagnosed with a very rare, very deadly form of bone and blood cancer, it was research that utilized horse antibodies that saved his life.

He is now 52 and cancer free for decades. We went out to check the horse ranches that used horses for this type of antibody collection. We made sure that every horse there was privately owned, and the owners could and did visit their horses on a regular, some daily basis, and that if the owners felt the horse was not being treated safely and humanely, they could take it home. Their own veterinarians could keep a careful watch on the horses. Few horses were ever utilized for more than a couple of times, to make sure they were not overused, or abused by the medical treatment needs. The antibody collection was basically an IV and then collection through blood, the same as a human donating blood. Their own veterinarian could watch them daily for bad reactions.

My younger son, a trainer at a young age, and I, trained horses for rescues and equine therapy programs for FREE. We also built a solid practice training expensive race, rodeo and show horses that for one reason or another had become so dangerously self protective they could not be raced, shown, or in competition. Our mentor trainers had told us, its great you can handle horses no one else can, but you have to learn to teach them to trust again and be safe around everyone for it to mean great training......and that is the skill we built.

Whether called out for a weanling, pampered and babied, that in six months was biting and kicking those who had loved it so.......no one could get near it, or get it out of a stall, into a trailer, or even out to the turn out corral or pasture, or back in........or a race, show or rodeo horse than usually one of the stall cleaning crew who had lied and was afraid of horses and beaten the horse with a rake, or shovel and created a monster that would not let anyone near it, we had built skill and retrained those horses and those that had to work with them. These are horses that will end up in the slaughter if not helped to trust humans, but not all of them again. That is a bit too much to ask. When you see an otherwise calm horse lay back its ears, and show its teeth, or even shriek a battle cry at the sight of certain handlers or trainers, you know exactly what happened to that horse when no one was looking. But, to get a new home when the show, racing or rodeo career is over, it became our duty to retrain them. I remember one trainer I had been talking to about a horse she had rescued after it was injured in a race, who said to me, I could tell the moment I put my hands on him that someone had loved him once. My son had trained that horse out after he had gotten so vicious and self protective he injured someone enough that the person passed away. He went on to become a children's show horse, and then jumper with his young owner, She had promised if she ever sold him, she would sell him to my son, he would have sold his truck, or his home to buy that horse, even if it was thirty. The young woman kept the horse his whole life. Sending pictures to my son from time to time.

Just because we were able to train in our manner, does not mean the general horse owner, or even trainer should attempt it. I am injured from being hit by drunk drivers who were racing, and know it is too dangerous for me to attempt that type of work again, but i have taught a couple of promising young trainers my lifework. Old horse trainers passed it along to me, and it is a duty to pass it along to people who will not get hurt doing this type of work.

Having said that, never think you know it all, I know I do not. The old horseman saying is "never a horseman couldn't be throwed, never a horse that couldn't be rode". And it often is the strangest thing. I trained stallions even my young athletic son was not able to train, horses prestigious trainers and turned down as too dangerous. I guess I was just too dumb to know ......or the horse just liked women more than men! There were horses that I had trouble with, that some of my youngest students got the best performance out of in shows and rodeos. Guess the horses liked kids better than know it all grown ups.

Chapter Two

. . . .

Animals and reality for you, for your children

I feel it is over -whelmingly important for people to realize that animals (all creatures of nature)are real, not toys, not tools and we owe them a duty to care for them humanely.

Every Native Nation has the DUTY to care for nature and the animals. There are many Native riders today, in all segments of the Americas, that "say" they are Native trainers, owners, or riders. They are not.

One weekend I attended the Spanish Horse Festival at the Equestrian Center in Los Angeles. There were some old men and women who DID ride in the ancient Native Nation styles of their own countries, Most of the others rode in a movie stereotype of abuse of the horses. Some were asked out of the event due to their "bits' being wrapped in barbed wire, or the high stepping feet of the horse having a barb shoved up into the frog of the foot to keep them high stepping.

I was talking to a middle aged man, he told he had gone to visit his Grandfather's ranch way back in the old country Mexico areas. He had been raised here in America with the movie inspired riders. He got up, big spurs, big whip, big mouth. The next thing he knew, his Grandfather had pulled a huge bull whip off the fence and snapped it out, grabbed him and tore him off the horse onto the ground. The Grandfather said, do NOT ever treat my horses or any horse in that disgusting way again.

He showed the then teen boy HOW to train and ride horses in their own ancient ways, NOT the abusive ways of the Spanish soldiers that had passed on and on in the Mission and cattle ranches of the Spanish land grant governors and land barons.

Over the course of this book I hope you will throw out all the movies and books, no matter how well meaning.....and learn to have some horse sense, and know that a horse is NOT a bicycle, it is a herd animal with a long memory that grieves for those it comes to trust and love, YOU.

Chance, this dog was given to us by a rescue, only skin and bones, left in a yard with no food, no water, and his chain tangled in a tree and piece of wire. When asked, his young teen owner said he was fine. When his Mom was asked, she said she had warned her son, and gave the $1500 dog, a new expensive dog house and pad, and dishes, asking someone recondition the dog and find it a forever home. Our vet called him "Second Chance" and he became "Chance" and a therapy dog for high risk youth.

. . . .

Chapter Three

ASK yourself and your children, how is a horse like a person, how is a horse different than a person.

IF you, or your child, think a horse is a tool, or a stuffed animal, it is NOT humane for you to buy a horse.

What exactly is the reason you want a horse, or want one for your child. List those reasons below and be honest.

IF your list does not contain the goal to be responsible for the lifetime (and not just euthanize it or send it to slaughter auction when you have your ribbons, or trophies, and trail riding satisfaction, do NOT buy a horse. IF you can NOT afford

GOOD, humane care for that horse, do not buy one. Children and teens often have whimsical ideas of what they want, it is NOT ok for you to give them the way to abuse and abandon an animal. I have rescued many in this situation, and either given them FOREVER homes, or made sure I put a 'return' to our program clause in any sale of a horse. I learned this when a friend donated her horse to a lovely religious equine therapy program following a divorce in which she lost the ability to care for her horse... They promised a forever home, she could visit, and return if they could not use the horse any longer. Instead she found they were going to sell the horse to the slaughter auction.

These kind and loving people said she had to meet the slaughter price, or that was that. She came over crying. I paid the money, and adopted the horse into our equine therapy program. She was beloved by students, probation and foster care group visitors and staff until she passed away surrounded by love at the age of 33. She was properly disposed of so the students could see what FOREVER means. Euthanized horses (she had fallen and injured herself in the bath rack and had to be put down) are filled with medications that make it illegal to dispose of them where pets or others might come in contact with the meat or hides

The first thing in all our classes is to ask everyone to tell us what is different, and what is the same about horses and humans.

We also ask our riders to bring a backpack and a huge bag of carrots, at least 25 pounds in the bag. We have our " want to be riders" put out an obstacle course, and then put that knapsack on and run that course at least two times. That is how much fun your horse has carrying you around.

A horse has hooves, we point out, and ask, do they have toes........ if a horse steps on the foot of another horse, it slides right off, if YOU step on the foot of a horse, it slides right off.

We ask the want to be riders......what about YOUR feet.....if a horse steps on YOUR toes, it does NOT slide right off. Do not wear steel toed shoes or boots, the weight of the horse will crush your feet inside the shoe, or boot and toes.

We ask, who is easier to get to understand reality....a horse to see you have toes, or YOU to get it, the horse does not have toes, does not see your toes and has no idea how to keep YOUR toes safe.

AND finally who is responsible for keeping your feet out from under those metal shod hooves?

TRAIN your horse to respect your space. A horse is a herd animal that knows the rules, and how to mind those rules. STAY out of my space, my silly long toes are there and I turn in to a nut, swearing and screaming when you are on my toes.

TRAIN yourself to respect your horse's space. Put a large soft drink cup between your eyes, THAT is what a horse sees. Horses have no need to see the ground, and in the wild their biggest activity is grazing. THEIR eyes see out the sides and can see movement. Their ears and noses pick up smells to let them know something dangerous might be coming into their space. They hear and smell things they can not see, their instinct says, kick it. Respect those metal shod feet when you come into their stalls, paddocks, or pastures. Let them know you are there.

LEARN what and where your horse sees. One of the biggest trusts you can build with your horse is to assure that YOU can see and are looking, seeing, and will protect that horse, and that STOP is a place with four hooves. planted on the ground until YOU say move and where and how fast to move.

These two points of forever respect are going to help you not get thrown from a horse protecting you and themselves from whatever it is a spooky horse is running from, and it is going to protect YOU from being kicked, bitten or trampled when your horse decides it is time to protect itself.

PEOPLE need to know a horse, not a wish or dream before buying one. Before buying, I suggest at least one full year of leasing a stable horse and making sure your lease says YOU clean and ready the horse for a ride, even if with a group trial or arena ride or lesson. YOU groom and bathe the horse. YOU make sure that horse is sound for the day's work before you take an unscheduled flying lesson because you did not notice a bite, kick, or back injury from rolling or rubbing around its own stall. AND YOU clean and care for the stall, learning exactly what that means and doing it every day, unless the horse is in a pasture, big enough that you only have to go through and pick up the manure, and put new dirt on the urine soaked places once or twice a week. The urine soaked manure packed into their feet is what causes the fungus to grow, stink, and destroy the feet of your horse. It is also what attracts flies. I learned that from the people we paid each month for fly protection. A horse ball laying around is not likely to bring flies, it is the urine ON that horse manure that helps the fly maggots to hatch, eat and grow.

Add to this, someone has to walk the pasture, or paddock fencing and watch carefully inside to make sure nothing is broken, fallen in, or dug up by horse hooves that is dangerous to the animals. This should be done at least three times a week.

Chapter Four

Clean Stalls, paddocks, pastures

For health, for safety, to stay out of trouble with animal rights and animal control officials.

As just noted in the last chapter, paddocks, pastures, and stalls, barns and pathways ALL have to be checked at least three times a week for loose boards, nails, holes dug by horse hooves, and anything else that can or "might" hurt a nosy horse. While small rocks and gravel do NOT harm horses as much as movies and story books alarm us, a horse can and will find the ONE rock, branch, or piece of ancient pipe buried in a pasture or arena. AND roll on it. This can and does cause serious, maybe even fatal injuries to the spine of the horse.

Loose eye hooks that people use to snap bungie cords onto need to be checked every time you use them, and as you unsnap the bungie or lead rope. I have seen expensive, winning race and show horses blinded by a bungee cord that either snapped out of the wall, or broke. Replace bungee cords often. Even if you are using them to hold things on the wall of the barn, or in a vehicle at the stable, they can, and DO snap back, or break and hit horses in the face or eyes.

Get into the habit of having a "fence tool" which is any type of fold up multi-tool you can carry about the barn in your pocket with your hoof pick. Another tool you NEED is a strong bolt cutter. In barns and stables that have any type of wire in the fences, especially chain link, which is NOT recommended by any trainer I know for areas horses are able to get their shod feet into.

GROOMING: this will be discussed later as an important part of the daily "what side of the barn"did the horse get up on, and KNOWING your horse so well, you can really tell when something is not right.

There are many myths out there about horse grooming. One is that the hair needs to be brushed the way it lays. Watch your horse roll, or rub body parts on fences, trees, and itching posts (you can find some great ideas for creating safe itching posts to keep your big best friend from ruining the fences and pushing down the trees and fence posts in your stable. In parks, or on rural trails, it may even mean a ticket and fine for YOU to allow you horse to rub on trees or sign and fence posts.

YOU, no matter how hard you try, are NOT going to rub the hair off your horse unless the hair is shedding, or something is wrong with the diet, or health of the horse.

General training at tracks (I was the assistant to the trainer who trained horse handlers for licensing at Santa Anita for some years) is to have a curry comb, and a brush in the other hand and work CIRCLES around the horse, from front to back. I always use a rubber curry glove in any place bones are likely to be disturbed by a hard curry comb or hard brush.

The hands cross over each other in these circles and as you get experience, you can easily groom a whole horse in less than ten minutes.

I do not use ties. At the tracks and most expensive show barns the horses have real humans hold them and the horses, no matter how young, are expected to stand on all four hooves through bathing, grooming and bandaging or putting on boots, etc.

This is because horses can and DO fall and get hurt while being tied. At most barns there is a ramped area with four stall mats that are cleaned and checked before and after each horse is bathed or groomed. A human handler helps that horse stay still.

Shoeing is often done in a nearby place, level and only one mat, the horse is expected to stand still on three or four legs and NOT touch the shoer for any reason.

Many farriers do NOT like owners, as opposed to experienced and trained horse handlers, to hold a horse for trims or shoes. ASK your shoer what is best for that professional you are trusting with your horse. DO NOT tell your shoer what the lady you met at the coffee shop had to say about this or that. IF in fact that lady is a shoer, hire her and do not tell her what your old shoer had to say about her.

I have seen heavy handed farriers that hit my horse, I fired them on the spot, one or more shoes pulled. One or more shoes trimmed. I do not hit my horses with files, or trimmers, I do not expect anyone to hit them with anything. HOWEVER, if my horse is kicking and putting the farriers at risk, and an open hand raps the horse, I keep my mouth shut and retrain my horse to be better behaved while having hoof care.

I have rescued horses that for a reason beyond the owners control, such as dying, and no one noticed the horses were not getting care except for feed thrown in during the funeral, etc... were left standing in a stall without clean bedding...big chunks of their hoof fell off when the shoes were pulled. It takes months and months to heal and regrow these hooves. Most people have the horses euthanized because they do not have the money, or the skill to help heal hooves. If these horses could stand patiently and calmly during their shoes being removed, and for the months of packing and hoof care, there is no excuse for your "baby" to not act properly when the horse shoer is working.

Stalls, paddocks.

If your horse is lucky enough to have an inside/outside stall and paddock, it has to be cleaned every single day, unless the paddock is fifty by fifty, then most humane societies say twice a week outside, and three times a week inside. BUT, if the horse leaves a lot of manure and urine inside, no animal control officer is going to believe you cleaned it three times a week, so plan on daily.

Most regulation size stall are required to be cleaned once a day. Many of the top trainers expect the grooms and hot walkers to toss manure out into the shed row if they see it, at any time of the day. The manure, crushed into the hoof with urine will cause fungus to grow, and skin disease to sprout quickly in those confined quarters.

It is YOUR choice, whether to use dirt, dirt and stall mats, (the dirt is usually purchased D and G sold especially for stalls) and/or shavings or straw. Look online, and ask your vet about what signs to look for....some horses are allergic to the shavings resins, and others eat the straw. It is up to YOU to decide how much shavings or straw you place on stall mats, or just dirt. BUT if you use either, YOU need to make sure it is cleaned properly every day or three times a week was your local humane society recommends.

Shavings and straw can be sprinkled in, or put in deep bedding. That is your choice. It is truly used to keep the horses clean more than comfy. Some race and show horses like to lie down or roll, or both after racing or performing......it will keep them cleaner if they have deep bedding. Stall mats, and a thorough check for holes that might be filled with urine UNDER the stall mats and bedding is necessary if you do not want to find a lot of maggots hiding out in your horses stall. Most big stables buy and keep large piles of properly mixed D and G to fill all holes and keep the stall level under the stall mat, or mats. (some people put in several mats to cover the entire stall under the bedding). This is more or less up to you as long as the mats are not used to hide urine puddles.

While I used to think a muddy horse was shameful, after I moved my horses to large pasture paddocks, and they rolled in the mud for fun. I changed my mind. Taking two or more hours to wash the mud off a horse completely rather than brush the horse down and ride is a choice trail riders often make. Do not judge others about their somewhat muddy horse as long as the areas under the saddle are cleaned of mud and grit so the horse is comfortable and not going to get saddle burns.

Horses can and DO live in backyards, in garages, in sheds in huge pastures......it is NONE of your business. YOU take care of your horse.

IF you do keep your horse in a garage, keep the car and motorized tools and vehicles outside. The gas smell is not great for horses, and it might cause a fire in which your horse could burn to death. If you keep your horse in stalls, or small paddocks, let them out to run in round corrals, or arenas. Train or ride them so they get exercise. In the wild horses often walk, trot and lope up to twenty miles a day.......your horse can walk a lot more miles than you can, so talk to your vet and set a pattern of daily exercise to keep your horse healthy.

Many people complain that their horse has sore legs, or feet, of course they do, you keep them in a box and come out on the weekend to be a weekend sports marathon rider. IF you do not have time for a horse at least three times a week, consider leasing a horse with someone else who does not have time either. The stables that own the horses will be grateful for the care the horses receive and when you can not come down to the stable someone else is there to take care of and ride or at least turn out the horse.

The proper way to clean a dirt stall is to pull the mat at least twice a week, put it outside and wash it and let it dry in the sun. These mats are VERY heavy. Go to the gym, you are going to need your arm strength. While the mat is drying rake the entire stall, remove all the manure, and if there is a big wet spot, shovel the mud out, replace it with clean D and G, when the mat is dry, put it in the stall, this is a good amount of time for your horse to have been in the round corral, or arena getting its own exercise. Make sure the waterer is working, and/or all feed tubs and buckets are cleaned and outside to dry with the mat in sunshine if possible. If your horse, or other horses are ill, clean as much as you can with a solution of hot water and bleach, runs and put in the sun to dry.

IF you are paying someone to clean the stall, and YOU put in mats, you need to negotiate and extra fee you can pay to have the mats pulled and cleaned properly.

Outside pipe corrals are most easily kept up if they are raked in fishbone pattern from a different side each day, and the holes filled as needed to keep urine puddles from forming.

THOSE automatic watering set ups. MAKE SURE THEY are cleaned at least twice a week with bleach and hot water, let the bleach mix sit three minutes or more, then rinse completely. On hot days, make sure the waterer is NOT filled with hot water.

Many times doing day or night watch at large stables or race tracks, or event centers, I have checked horses, they are dehydrated, so I check the waterer. The piping is along a wall OUTSIDE, in full sun, the water is TOO HOT for the horse to drink. Fix it, or buy and hang water buckets inside the stalls on hot days. Some stables have put padding to keep the sun off the pipes, others have had the whole piping system changed so it is INSIDE the barn, NOT out in the hot sun.

Many horses in outdoor paddocks, or pastures with automatic watering systems do NOT realize that at least part of hot days the water in the bowls is too hot for the horses to drink. There are some great big auto-watering systems with big, deep receptacles for the water to fill and remain cool all day. In the same thought, many automatic watering systems FREEZE in cold weather, the horses are forced to attempt to lick the ice in order to get some water, certainly not enough for a horse, no matter what the weather. Before leaving big stables, I did a night check, often I found horses dehydrated, their waterer broken. If left all night they are at risk for colic. BE sure YOU check your horses water, and ask the vet to show you how to tell when the horse is dehydrated.

Chapter Five

. . . .

FEED

Ask your vet, not "someone" or "someone's friend"

Horses eat "like a horse". It is up to you to make sure what they eat is healthy, and clean, and FOR horses. Horses love treats, people will tell you that they feed their horses all kinds of strange things. It does NOT mean it is good for horses because their particular horse did not get sick, and/or die.

Many a vet will tell you that some new horse owner has figured out that hay is cheaper at some feed stores. The feed stores do NOT all have signs up that say "this hay is for goats" or "this hay is for cows", yes, horse hay is more expensive, but your horse dying, a horrible death, and/or big vet bills make it well worth the price.

Every horse owner you can find will have their own favorites of supplements, and additional feeds or pellets. ASK YOUR VET, and do what the vet says for your horse. IF you trust the little old lady down the street more than your vet, and the closest she has ever come to a horse is watching horse racing on television, but "knows someone" who has a horse.........get a new vet that you trust.

Some horses have allergies. Some horses are prone to fat, some horses can eat like two horses and remain thin......there might be reasons for all of this and the vet needs to know, and HELP you keep your horse healthy. Just turning them out on grass sounds nice, but wild horses scamper over twenty or more acres of land each day and pick among many plants and weeds as well as grasses to keep their weight and health strong. And many of them die.

I personally like to give my horses as much of natural experience as possible and asked my vets, they said Bermuda grass. SO, I buy it, and try and keep some available at all times to all the horses, whether stalled, or out in pasture. Some people say, the horse will get a grass belly. IF I follow the vet's instructions on other hays, and supplements I have not had that problem, but it does give the horses a nice munch available all day long. I only pull the Bermuda before events or races as directed by the vet.

If the vet approves, an active horse has a hay rack in the stall that has three way, alfalfa mix and a specified amount of cubes and pellets with supplements and oil added if the vet agrees. Less active horses have their own blends for one meal a day, a second meal as the vet recommends, and their Bermuda. Many trainers prefer Timothy plus the three way in the free feed hay rack. I am allergic to Timothy and get hives, so prefer to avoid it.

Other trainers have different favorites. As long as the vet approves, and it is working for the horse, that is fine.

Chapter Six

Daily health and injury check

*What side of the stall did your horse wake up on this morning.....
it can save you vet bills, a dead horse, and /or an unscheduled
flying lesson*

*Through decades of working in huge racing environments and
show, or rodeo environments I have seen proof of something
some of the old trainers had told me when I was a child, learning
to ride and working in stables to get to ride. I have noticed a
horse that just seemed "off" to me or seemed ill or injured being
led out for training, or racing, rodeo, or show events.*

*I was not surprised how, over the decades, my viewpoint was
proven when the horse was injured, blew up, or collapsed.*

*CHECK your horse, as you get to know your horse more and
more, it will almost be like your own body as you groom, run
your hands over in final inspection, put on boots, clean hooves,
or put a saddle or bridle on that horse. A small flinch, that no
one but you might notice will lead to a day off, or a vet seeing
the animal if needed.*

*On the other hand, many people own old, or rescued horses
that have old injuries that the vet knows well, and does NOT*

harm the horse to continue to work without further treatment. I rescued an old mare, I knew her one, all her life owner, the horse limped from what was diagnosed and watched by the vet as a mid-level arthritis, not rare for an animal that age. People thought I was mean, or should have her put down if they saw me lead her out to the arena, or just let her go in the pasture to graze awhile. After her medication and the sun helped her, she was happy to be groomed, bathed, and work with new riders learning how to do these tasks, and how to saddle, bridle, and put on bandaging and boots, clean feet, or pack hooves. She was fine until the next morning when she limped out to greet a new day. Another of the horses that lived well into her thirties, beloved and loving in our equine therapy programs.

LEARN your own horse. If the horse suddenly refuses the bit, or snaps at you while grooming any area, go over it and if necessary ask the vet to drop by and take a look. A horse fine one day, may have bitten something while eating over night, and chipped a tooth, or loosened it, and the bit is not going to be a pleasant, or safe experience until the tooth is dealt with.

LEARN how to manage braiding. Some horses have long manes and tails, they stay cleaner and healthier if braided properly, loosely, but have to be brushed out and reset daily. Braids, especially tight show braids, if slept on, or rubbed on the stall walls or doorway can leave you horse without a mane or tail, or with big chunks falling out when you get around to taking out the braids and combing out the hair.

Feet and legs need to be carefully cleaned and gone over each day before and after a ride, or turn out. Hooves need to be picked, brushed, and either lotion or oil put on the each hoof as your vet recommends. Fungus medications need to be applied as the vet recommends. Some horses never seem to get hoof disease, or rot, other horses can, and DO get really severe infections in a day or two.

IF you have a young horse, or a foal with its Mother, still pick up its feet, tap them and rub them with your hand from the second or third day after foaling. Rub the legs, and by six months bandage the mare, then the young horse. Make your own SHORT bandages and start with one leg only, work up to all four. You will more than likely never have problems with that horse over hoof, or leg cleaning or treatments. The Mare is the best trainer for young horses. I noticed that my foals watch their Mother and readily accept what she has allowed. I use a tiny racing saddle, and by six months put a saddle pad, and the tiny racing saddle on the foal. From time to time over the next three years, I do the same. Most mares I have worked with, if allowed to keep their own timetable, will demand their child stay away, not nurse, and it is time to move the young horse to its own stall.......Many foals are taken early, put in pastures with other weanlings, or same age groups and often (if racing horses intended to race) are already sent to the track in their second year of life.....I have found it leads to horses not knowing many of the good habits of horses, and some not even knowing they are horses, they are a strange eighteen hundred pound spoiled child. If at all possible, let your Mare raise and train her foal WITH you. I do NOT tie young horses, or do many of the mean, and sad things I have seen people do saying they are "imprinting". Be careful who you follow or learn from. ALL foals should be ready for a complete daily health inspection, and grooming, bathing, by six months old. ASK your vet and the farrier when the first trim should occur. Sometimes leg or hoof deformities can be corrected early if taken care of by a corrective farrier and your vet.

A six month old foal should readily accept a rubber bit, halter, leading, and saddle, blankets of all types. All four feet cleaned and brushed, tap the hooves with the brush so the horse is not shocked when the farrier comes along one day and taps and cuts on the hooves.

Chapter Seven

Riding, showing, etc

Making sure you choose the right horse for the right job, and make forever plans for that horse if it does not work out.

One of the hardest parts of being a trainer is to have someone bring a horse to you, and with heartfelt joy ask you to make their dream come true. A nice plow or draft show horse is NOT going to win the Kentucky Derby, or a jumping competition.

A high spirited Arabian is not going to be a great trail horse for a green teenage rider.

A rider who is green, green, green, is not going to win a three day event at a national horse show, no matter how expensive the horse, or how well trained it was before it was purchased.

DO NOT BUY a horse, for yourself, or your child, that is just too much horse for riding skill and experience.

SPEAKING OF GREEN:

A horse is green, green, green when it has less than 500 RIDING hours, NOT in the pen, or you owned it more than 500 hours, or you paid 500 trainers to train that horse.

A horse becomes GREEN when it has 500 solid safe riding hours to start its career.

A person, also is green, green, green with less than 500 GOOD riding hours. This does not mean to on 25 20 hour weekends riding the horses in the round corral.

Remember, as some famous trainers say, PERFECT practice. NOT just being out there doing the wrong thing, you NEED 500 solid hours of green, green, green to become green.

A green horse and a green rider is a prescription for injury or death.

Forget the movies, the horse stories you read as a child, and what some woman you know has to say.

A woman came to a riding program I had been asked to teach after the regular teacher had to resign when her husband had heart surgery and she needed to take care of him. This woman had a young daughter. The woman also had some unfulfilled dream of her own of being the best horsewoman of the world, and refused to look at reality.

I told her that MY way was to evaluate every rider and let them move along as I saw safe for the rider and the horses.

The woman had a tantrum, in front of all those other children and their parents.

I had the lead rope of a horse that her daughter had wanted to ride, but I felt was way to much for a six year old. The woman was threatening and assaultive, so I kept the horses between us.

One day not long after I saw "something" lying in the street as I drove up to my stable. The something turned out to be that child. Her mother had gone out and purchased a horse for her, taken her to the park to ride and let her ride up the street alone. The minute the horse realized it was on the way home, it began to gallop. The horse tripped over a curb and the child was flung, full speed on to the roadway. The owner of the house had been in his front yard and seen it all. He also was an off duty police officer and had called an ambulance. The child had not moved, but was breathing. The mother was crying and trying to run up the steep hill, useless to help her daughter blocks away in the street, OR the loose horse galloping on asphalt to its stable (asphalt or cement require special shoes and boots or leg bones

- 42 -

split, often unnoticed and either kill the horse, or take months to heal).

DO NOT LET THIS HAPPEN TO YOU. Whether you or your child, know HOW to ride, how to handle any situation with a horse, such as get off and walk it home if necessary.......and how to get off a horse at walk, trot, canter and full gallop safely. Most trainers say never get off. Better to walk and live another day than to die or be crippled for life.

The child survived, but they sold that poor horse and the kid never rode again. If YOU wanted a horse when you were five, YOU go take riding lessons and horse care lessons until a reputable trainer says you are ready to move up, and/or to horse ownership.

Chapter Eight

. . . .

All other animals, fish, fowl, etc.

These are not toys, you can NOT just put them in the closet, or the garage and forget about them. Children need to sign commitments to care for them.

YOU need to talk to the teacher, and other relatives before you decide to give your child even a goldfish, or a little hamster in a cage.

NEVER start with a horse. Horses are expensive and need FOREVER homes. Dogs, cats, and other animals ALL deserve love, care, NO abuse, and forever homes. If you let your fifteen year old get a dog, that young person is going to get a boy or girl friend, go to college, or get into a business....YOU are going to end up owning a pet that does NOT understand where the love of its life has gone.

ASK yourself: does my child clean up after themself in the kitchen, bathroom, living room, or yard.

Does my child do their homework consistently and on time without me reminding or nagging?

Does my child get to school on time, daily without having to be nagged?

If the answer to any of these questions is NO, then your child is NOT ready for a pet, and certainly not for a horse.

Get them a nice bike.

CARE of a horse

Horses require daily and routine care which is expensive. HIRING a person does NOT excuse you from making sure the animal is properly cared for at all times.

A HORSE needs to be checked each morning. IF at a stable, or before work you have to find out if they check them, or if YOU (and your child) need a NEW schedule to stop and check the horse BEFORE your day gets going.

If the horse is at your home, YOU and your child need to check that horse BEFORE your shower or breakfast. There is no need to put on your work suit, if you are going to spend the next few hours waiting for the vet and caring for a sick horse, or waiting for the horse ambulance to come or the horse coroner to pick up the body if it dies or has to be put down.

Depending on your vet approved feeding schedule the horse needs food. Check the water. Bucket or watering system, be sure there is good clean water.

Exercise.

Whether turned out or exercised or ridden a horse needs exercise. The solid rule is: for every. minute cantered, an HOUR of cool down, turn out, etc to avoid colic.

IF for some reason you gallop your horse, or it. has gotten loose and galloped home from trail for park........it takes up to FOUR hours of proper walking (no water, and then air temperature NOT cold, until you feel the chest and the horse is cooled enough to have. TWO sips). CHILDREN can not pull horses. away from cold water fast enough, they can and often do, colic and die from too much. cold water before cooled properly. When cool enough (ask your vet) bathe the hot horse, and either walk it out, or let it finish cooling in a round corral, or arena before putting in to feed.

. . . .

FOREVER, makes plans in case YOU do not make it to forever.

Make sure ALL your animals will be taken care of, even if you pay a rescue to come and pick them up as noted in your will. You will learn some great clues on preparing for your loss for your children in this chapter as well.

Death, or disability, especially our own, is not a happy subject.

IF you have children, or pets, you NEED to make sure you have a will, a trust, and trusted people to take care of all that you will no longer be able to do if disabled, or passed away.

GET death and disability insurance to cover your responsibilities include the cost in the cost for a child, pet, or horse.

IF you do not want your ex to get custody of your child, you may not legally be able to do much except put this in a will, and list the real reasons. I hate ....since our divorce is not a real reason. My ex.........is in prison, and has drug abuse issues IS a real issue that a judge can look at to decide custody of your child.

APPOINT a legal guardian. Someone who will make sure your child is being well cared for, or will contact the judge.

APPOINT a separate financial guardian if necessary. An unrelated law firm, if need be, to make sure your money is not going to be gambled, or used to pay for things that are NOT for your child's best interest. Start an academic account for each child, that can NOT be used except for one period of college or technical school at a time. IF your child does not maintain a passing grade level, the financial aid will NOT be given again until ONE successful quarter, or half has been accomplished and the financial guardian gets the judge to say it is OK to start funding of education again.

The same is a good plan for your horse, pets, and even yourself should you be disabled. Have a support system set up. There are horse ranches that will take annual payments for your horse to be turned out and taken care of for life. There are other equine retirement programs that care for the horse or do NOT get the monthly payments from your estate.

You might ask a family member or friend to be the guardian of your horse, and leave a financial estate to pay for the needs of the horse. ASK the person before the need arises.

Make a plan.

Chapter Ten

CLOSING

The PEOPLE of the United States have created laws, and agencies to make sure that animals are cared for.

International animal rights groups are there to find the worst offenders and make sure the public knows they are there, and NOT being subject to the law.

Especially those who make money off the sale of animals, fish, birds, reptiles and even plants that can and DO cause harm to other animals and plants need to be regulated.

Old Granny with her little pot of favorites, sneaking them in in her luggage has been THE biggest cause of huge infestations of both animals, and plants across America.

Google these problems and study them WITH your child before you help them, or yourself to avoid the laws.

Vaccines and veterinarian clearance before moving animals prevents these problems. I personally have worked at the tracks when huge pandemics of expensive and cared for horses have occurred, it is shocking and heartbreaking to see the suffering and death of the track animals, and any other animal that has come in contact with the virus, or bacteria that was brought in by selfish and corrupt persons who did not get vaccines, or proper veterinarian clearance before shipping animals around a State, or from State to State, or from other Nations.

As sick and sorry as all this is, we work with CHILDREN, soldiers, first responders, and seniors who have been abandoned, neglected and/or abused. BEFORE you decide to buy yourself, or your child a horse (or any animals) make sure you are capable of offering it a forever home. The stories of animals (and children) are few and far between. Many people want to say "OH I know....." it is NOT the norm, and it is NOT reality. Most large animals that are abandoned or neglected end up in slaughter sales, shoved head to rear, squeezed in to trucks, *often with a second row above them, urinating and excreting on them before being dumped at a slaughter plant, often in other countries where the laws are not there to protect the animals.*

Humans can do a better job, for animals, this planet, and each other. God bless.

Teaching a child about animals and their rights

Whether you believe in the ethical treatment or animals or not, it is important for you to learn the rights of not just animals, and to teach your child the rights of other creatures, including humans.

Horses are herd animals. Dogs are pack animals, they become confused and broken hearted to lose their herd or pack.

BEFORE giving a horse to your child, or allowing some "kind hearted" person to push their old, unwanted horse on your child, make sure you and your child understand what a FOREVER home is about.

Chapter Eight
. . . .

BEFORE, you, or your child buys a horse.....

How to set a one year (at least) plan to decide if you really want to buy a horse, or to allow your child to buy one. Remember that YOU as the adult, are legally liable for the care of the animal you allow your child to have.

After you have listened to what it is YOU or your child wants, it is time to form a plan and to look at that wish to see if it is reasonable.

Look at the pile of toys in the closet, broken, dirty, not cared for. At one time your child HAD TO HAVE. Look at the pile of shoes and clothing on your own closet floor, or in a bag in the garage to go to the Goodwill. Look at the exercise equipment and bikes in your garage, covered with dust, knocked over and left to lay on the floor.

Each of these THINGS was once something YOU yourself wanted, or wanted to provide to your child.

Look at the empty fish bowls, aquariums and pots, and containers for long dead plants that were never planted, or not properly cared for in your yard.

Each of these things is a THING.

A fish, dog, or horse is NOT a bicycle, or even a plant, left to suffer and die. Or to be abused by a child, or adult who has no clue as to how to care for that animal.

We all see the commercials for the animal rescues and ASPCA and watch the series of television shows about people who rescue unwanted and/or neglected and abused animals. DO NOT ALLOW YOURSELF (or yourself through your child) to become one of the abusive owners. If not humane enough to care for the animals, remember often it is a crime to abuse or neglect an animal you are legally responsible for. As noted above, parents are going to be held LEGALLY responsible for abuse and neglect of their children's animals. While sitting in jail, paying lawyers, and fines, remember....you made your child happy, and an animal suffer.

ONE major argument often heard is that "in the old days" on the farm, rancho, or in the old country.........animals were treated differently . In the "old country" in the "old days" people lived on huge open acreage where a dog might catch its own meals, an eagle, or owl, coyote or wolf might eat unwanted pups, and horses could browse around and find something to eat. Wolves and mountain lions killed injured or old horses, they were not starving and suffering because your child got tired of them.

That is NOT America today. It is not any city in the world today. IF you allow your household to become responsible for an animals (or child) take proper care of it, and make sure it will have a forever home. The quaint stories of people who rescue are few and far between. Watch ANY animal rescue program and you will hear how sad they are that they can not care for more than the small number of animals they care for and try to find forever homes to love and give the rescued animals homes. MOST unwanted and neglected animals end up in pounds, euthanized, and big animals sold at the slaughter auctions after they fail to sell at the pound auctions.

YOU and your child need to understand, an unwanted bike can be given to the thrift shops, or sold by the dump to metal salvaging companies to become part of a new car, refrigerator, or can of some kind. An animal will be afraid, suffer and die due to YOUR negligence and lack of care.

. . . .

FOREVER HOMES

How To bring peace and forever to your animals, children and family members.

This is a short lesson.

To bring peace and forever to your home, children and pets, make sure YOU know and then teach your children the difference between a "thing" and a living being.

Make sure YOU know, and teach your. children and pets to love and respect one another.

Volunteer for rescues with your children, and learn the realities of even taking care of a plant, and each other before introducing pets into your family.

Chapter Ten

. . . .

Other animals, and eventually your grandchildren.

Bring up a child ......

As the twig is bent, so grows the tree.....The teaching chapter Proverbs of the Bible, as well as any gardening book teaches this reality.

One day, you will be a Grandparent. THIS is the time to teach your child the patience, self-less care, and ability to know what is a need, and what is just a want. OR you will be taking your child to Court, or a social worker will be at your door, to tell YOU to take care of your Grandchildren because you did NOT teach your child that living beings deserve best. of forever homes.

Chapter Eleven

. . . .

Closing

All of our group of books, and workbooks contain some work pages, and/or suggestions for the reader, and those teaching these books to make notes, to go to computer, and libraries and ask others for information to help these projects work their best.

To utilize these to their fullest, make sure YOU model the increased thoughts and availability of more knowledge to anyone you share these books and workbooks with in classes, or community groups.

Magazines are, as noted in most of the books, a wonderful place to look for and find ongoing research and information. Online search engines often bring up new research in the areas, and newly published material.

We all have examples of how we learned and who it was that taught us.

One of the strangest lessons I have learned was walking to a shoot in downtown Los Angeles. The person who kindly told me to park my truck in Pasadena, and take the train had been unaware that the weekend busses did NOT run early in the morning when the crews had to be in to set up. That person, being just a participant, was going much later in the day, taking a taxi, and had no idea how often crews do NOT carry purses with credit cards, large amounts of cash, and have nowhere to carry those items, because the crew works hard, and fast during a set up and tear down and after the shoot are TIRED and not looking to have to find items that have been left around, or stolen.

As I walked, I had to travel through an area of Los Angeles that had become truly run down and many homeless were encamped about and sleeping on the sidewalks and in alleys. I saw a man, that having worked in an ER for many years I realized was DEAD. I used to have thoughts about people who did not notice people needing help, I thought, this poor man, this is probably the most peace he has had in a long time. I prayed for him and went off to my unwanted walk across town. As I walked, I thought about myself, was I just heartless, or was I truly thinking this was the only moment of peace this man had had for a long time and just leaving him to it. What good were upset neighbors, and police, fire trucks and ambulances going to do. He was calmly, eyes open, staring out at a world that had failed him while alive, why rush to disturb him now that nothing could be done.

I did make sure he was DEAD. He was, quite cold rigid.

I learned that day that it is best to do what a person needs, NOT what we need.

Learning is about introspection and grounding of material. Passing little tests on short term memory skills and not knowing what it all means is NOT education, or teaching.

As a high school student, in accelerated Math and Science programs, in which I received 4.0 grades consistently, I walked across a field, diagonally, and suddenly all that math and science made sense, it was not just exercises on paper I could throw answers back on paper, but I realized had NO clue as to what it all really meant.

OTHER BOOKS by this author, and team

Most, if not all, of these books are written at a fourth grade level. First, the author is severely brain damaged from a high fever disease caused by a sample that came in the mail, without a warning that it had killed during test marketing. During the law suit, it was discovered that the corporation had known prior to mailing out ten million samples, WITHOUT warnings of disease and known deaths, and then NOT telling anyone after a large number of deaths around the world started. Second, the target audience is high risk youth, and young veterans, most with a poor education before signing into, or being drafted into the military as a hope Many of our veterans are Vietnam or WWII era.

Maybe those recruiting promises would come true. They would be trained, educated, and given chance for a home, and to protect our country and its principles. Watch the movies Platoon, and Born on the Fourth of July as well as the Oliver Stone series on history to find out how these dreams were meet.

DO NOT bother to write and tell us of grammar or spelling errors. We often wrote these books and workbooks fast for copyrights. We had learned our lessons about giving our material away when one huge charity asked us for our material, promising a grant, Instead, we heard a couple of years later they had built their own VERY similar project, except theirs charged for services, ours were FREE, and theirs was just for a small group, ours was training veterans and others to spread the programs as fast as they could.. They got a Nobel Peace prize. We keep saying we are not bitter, we keep saying we did not do our work to get awards, or thousands of dollars of grants....but, it hurts. Especially when lied to and that group STILL sends people to US for help when they can not meet the needs, or the veterans and family can not afford their "charitable" services. One other group had the nerve to send us a Cease and Desist using our own name. We said go ahead and sue, we have proof of legal use of this name for decades. That man had the conscience to apologize, his program was not even FOR veterans or first responders, or their families, nor high risk kids. But we learned. Sometimes life is very unfair.

We got sued again later for the same issue. We settled out of Court as our programs were just restarting and one of the veterans said, let's just change that part of the name and keep on training veterans to run their own programs. Smart young man.

Book List:

DRAGON KITES and other stories:

The Grandparents Story list will add 12 new titles this year. We encourage every family to write their own historic stories. That strange old Aunt who when you listen to her stories left a rich and well regulated life in the Eastern New York coastal fashionable families to learn Telegraph messaging and go out to the old west to LIVE her life. That old Grandfather or Grandmother who was sent by family in other countries torn by war to pick up those "dollars in the streets" as noted in the book of that title.

Books in publication, or out by summer 2021

Carousel Horse: A Children's book about equine therapy and what schools MIGHT be and are in special private programs.

Carousel Horse: A smaller version of the original Carousel Horse, both contain the workbooks and the screenplays used for on site stable programs as well as lock down programs where the children and teens are not able to go out to the stables.

Spirit Horse II: This is the work book for training veterans and others interested in starting their own Equine Therapy based programs. To be used as primary education sites, or for supplementing public or private school programs. One major goal of this book is to copyright our founding material, as we gave it away freely to those who said they wanted to help us get grants. They did not. Instead they built their own programs, with grant money, and with donations in small, beautiful stables and won....a Nobel Peace Prize for programs we invented. We learned our lessons, although we do not do our work for awards, or grants, we DO not like to be ripped off, so now we copyright.

Reassessing and Restructuring Public Agencies; This book is an over view of our government systems and how they were expected to be utilized for public betterment. This is a Fourth Grade level condemnation of a PhD dissertation that was not accepted be because the mentor thought it was "against government" .. The first paragraph noted that a request had been made, and referrals given by the then White House.

Reassessing and Restructuring Public Agencies; TWO. This book is a suggestive and creative work to give THE PEOPLE the idea of taking back their government and making the money spent and the agencies running SERVE the PEOPLE ;not politicians. This is NOT against government, it is about the DUTY of the PEOPLE to oversee and control government before it overcomes us.

Could This Be Magic? A Very Short Book. This is a very short book of pictures and the author's personal experiences as the Hall of Fame band VAN HALEN practiced in her garage. The pictures are taken by the author, and her then five year old son. People wanted copies of the pictures, and permission was given to publish them to raise money for treatment and long term Veteran homes.

Carousel TWO: Equine therapy for Veterans. publication pending 2021

Carousel THREE: Still Spinning: Special Equine therapy for women veterans and single mothers. This book includes TWELVE STEPS BACK FROM BETRAYAL for soldiers who have been sexually assaulted in the active duty military and help from each other to heal, no matter how horrible the situation. publication pending 2021

LEGAL ETHICS: AN OXYMORON. A book to give to lawyers and judges you feel have not gotten the justice of American Constitution based law (Politicians are great persons to gift with this book). Publication late 2021

PARENTS CAN LIVE and raise great kids.

Included in this book are excerpts from our workbooks from KIDS ANONYMOUS and KIDS JR, and A PARENTS PLAIN RAP (to teach sexuality and relationships to their children. This program came from a copyrighted project thirty years ago, which has been networked into our other programs. This is our training work book. We asked AA what we had to do to become a real Twelve Step program as this is considered a quasi twelve step program children and teens can use to heal BEFORE becoming involved in drugs, sexual addiction, sexual trafficking and relationship woes, as well as unwanted, neglected and abused or having children murdered by parents not able to deal with the reality of parenting. Many of our original students were children of abuse and neglect, no matter how wealthy. Often the neglect was by society itself when children lost parents to illness, accidents or addiction. We were told, send us a copy and make sure you call it quasi. The Teens in the first programs when surveyed for the outcome research reports said, WE NEEDED THIS EARLIER. SO they helped younger children invent KIDS JR. Will be republished in 2021 as a documentary of the work and success of these projects.

Addicted To Dick. This is a quasi Twelve Step program for women in domestic violence programs mandated by Courts due to repeated incidents and danger, or actual injury or death of their children.

Addicted to Dick 2018 This book is a specially requested workbook for women in custody, or out on probation for abuse to their children, either by themselves or their sexual partners or spouses. The estimated national number for children at risk at the time of request was three million across the nation. During

Covid it is estimated that number has risen. Homelessness and undocumented families that are unlikely to be reported or found are creating discussion of a much larger number of children maimed or killed in these domestic violence crimes. THE most important point in this book is to force every local school district to train teachers, and all staff to recognize children at risk, and to report their family for HELP, not punishment. The second most important part is to teach every child on American soil to know to ask for help, no matter that parents, or other relatives or known adults, or unknown adults have threatened to kill them for "telling". Most, if not all paramedics, emergency rooms, and police and fire stations are trained to protect the children and teens, and get help for the family.. PUNISHMENT is not the goal, eliminating childhood abuse and injury or death at the hands of family is the goal of all these projects. In some areas JUDGES of child and family courts were taking training and teaching programs themselves to HELP. FREE..

Addicted to Locker Room BS. This book is about MEN who are addicted to the lies told in locker rooms and bars. During volunteer work at just one of several huge juvenile lock downs, where juveniles who have been convicted as adults, but are waiting for their 18th birthday to be sent to adult prisons, we noticed that the young boys and teens had "big" ideas of themselves, learned in locker rooms and back alleys. Hundreds of these young boys would march, monotonously around the enclosures, their lives over. often facing long term adult prison sentences.

The girls, we noticed that the girls, for the most part were smart, had done well in school, then "something" happened. During the years involved in this volunteer work I saw only ONE young girl who was so mentally ill I felt she was not reachable, and should be in a locked down mental health facility for help; if at all possible, and if teachers, and others had been properly trained, helped BEFORE she gotten to that place, lost in the horror and broken of her childhood and early teen years.

We noticed that many of the young women in non military sexual assault healing programs were "betrayed" in many ways, by step fathers, boyfriends, even fathers, and mothers by either molestation by family members, or allowing family members or friends of parents to molest these young women, often as small children. We asked military sexually assaulted young women to begin to volunteer to help in the programs to heal the young girls and teens, it helped heal them all.

There was NOTHING for the boys that even began to reach them until our research began on the locker room BS theory of life destruction and possible salvaging by the boys themselves, and men in prisons who helped put together something they thought they MIGHT have heard before they ended up in prison.

Americans CAN Live Happily Ever After. Parents edition.One

Americans CAN Live Happily Ever After. Children's edition Two.

Americans CAN Live Happily Ever After. Three. After Covid. This book includes "Welcome to America" a requested consult workbook for children and youth finding themselves in cages, auditoriums on cots, or in foster group homes or foster care of relatives or non-relatives with NO guidelines for their particular issues. WE ASKED the kids, and they helped us write this fourth grade level workbook portion of this book to help one another and each other. Written in a hurry! We were asked to use our expertise in other youth programs, and our years of experience teaching and working in high risk youth programs to find something to help.

REZ CHEESE Written by a Native American /WASP mix woman. Using food, and thoughts on not getting THE DIABETES, stories are included of a childhood between two worlds.

REZ CHEESE TWO A continuation of the stress on THE DIABETES needing treatment and health care from birth as well as recipes, and stories from Native America, including thoughts on asking youth to help stop the overwhelming numbers of suicide by our people.

BIG LIZ: LEADER OF THE GANG Stories of unique Racial Tension and Gang Abatement projects created when gangs and racial problems began to make schools unsafe for our children.

DOLLARS IN THE STREETS, ghost edited for author Lydia Caceras, the first woman horse trainer at Belmont Park.

95 YEARS of TEACHING:

A book on teaching, as opposed to kid flipping

Two teachers who have created and implemented systems for private and public education a combined 95 plus years of teaching talk about experiences and realities and how parents can get involved in education for their children. Included are excerpts from our KIDS ANONYMOUS and KIDS JR workbooks of over 30 years of free youth programs.

A HORSE IS NOT A BICYCLE. A book about pet ownership and how to prepare your children for responsible pet ownership and along the way to be responsible parents. NO ONE needs to own a pet, or have a child, but if they make that choice, the animal, or child deserves a solid, caring forever home.

OLD MAN THINGS and MARE'S TALES. this is a fun book about old horse trainers I met along the way. My husband used to call the old man stories "old man things", which are those enchanting and often very effective methods of horse, pet, and even child rearing. I always said I brought up my children and my students the same as I had trained horses and dogs......I meant that horses and dogs had taught me a lot of sensible, humane ways to bring up an individual, caring, and dream realizing adult who was HAPPY and loved.

STOP TALKING, DO IT

ALL of us have dreams, intentions, make promises. This book is a workbook from one of our programs to help a person make their dreams come true, to build their intentions into goals, and realities, and to keep their promises. One story from this book, that inspired the concept is a high school kid, now in his sixties, that was in a special ed program for drug abuse and not doing well in school. When asked, he said his problem was that his parents would not allow him to buy a motorcycle. He admitted that he did not have money to buy one, insure one, take proper driver's education and licensing examinations to own one, even though he had a job. He was asked to figure out how much money he was spending on drugs. Wasting his own money, stealing from his parents and other relatives, and then to figure out, if he saved his own money, did some side jobs for neighbors and family until he was 18, he COULD afford the motorcycle and all it required to legally own one. In fact, he did all, but decided to spend the money on college instead of the motorcycle when he graduated from high school. His priorities had changed as he learned about responsible motorcycle ownership and risk doing the assignments needed for his special ed program. He also gave up drugs, since his stated reason was he could not have a motorcycle, and that was no longer true, he COULD have a motorcycle, just had to buy it himself, not just expect his parents to give it to him.

Printed in the United States
by Baker & Taylor Publisher Services